D0911498

A FUNNY THING HAPPENED
ON THE WAY TO THE FORUM

Music and Lyrics by
STEPHEN SONDHEIM

Book by
BURT SHEVELOVE and LARRY GELBART
based on the plays of Plautus

Vocal Score

Piano reduction by
ROBERT H. NOELTNER

BURTHEN MUSIC COMPANY, INC.
Sole selling agent: CHAPPELL & CO., INC.

to Oscar Hammerstein II

A FUNNY THING HAPPENED
ON THE WAY TO THE FORUM

Produced by HAROLD PRINCE. First performance May 8, 1962
at the Alvin Theatre, New York

Production Directed by GEORGE ABBOTT

Choreography & Musical Staging by JACK COLE
Settings and Costumes by TONY WALTON
Lighting by JEAN ROSENTHAL
Musical Direction by HAROLD HASTINGS
Orchestrations by IRWIN KOSTAL & SID RAMIN
Dance Music arranged by HAL SCHAEFER

Cast of Characters
(In order of appearance)

PROLOGUS	Zero Mostel
THE PROTEANS	Eddie Phillips, George Reeder, David Evans
SENEX, *a citizen of Rome*	David Burns
DOMINA, *his wife*	Ruth Kobart
HERO, *his son*	Brian Davies
HYSTERIUM, *slave to Senex and Domina*	Jack Gilford
LYCUS, *a dealer in courtesans*	John Carradine
PSEUDOLUS, *slave to Hero*	Zero Mostel
TINTINNABULA	Roberta Keith
PANACEA	Lucienne Bridou
THE GEMINAE	Lisa James, Judy Alexander
VIBRATA	Myrna White
GYMNASIA	Gloria Kristy
PHILIA	Preshy Marker
ERRONIUS, *a citizen of Rome*	Raymond Walburn
MILES GLORIOSUS, *a warrior*	Ronald Holgate

THE TIME: 200 years before the Christian era, a day in Spring
THE PLACE: a street in Rome, in front of the houses of Erronius, Senex, and Lycus
THE ACTION is continuous.

Instrumentation

WOODWIND No. 1:   Flute/Clarinet/Alto Saxophone
No. 2:   Clarinet/Alto Saxophone
No. 3:   Clarinet/Tenor Saxophone
No. 4:   Bass Clarinet/Baritone Saxophone
No. 5:   *Optional* Clarinet/Flute

3 Trumpets, 3 Trombones (2nd-3rd *optional*), 1 or 2 Percussion, Piano, *optional* Harp
6 Violins, 2 Violas, 2 Violoncellos, 1 Contrabass

Musical Program

ACT I.

No.   *page*

1. Overture 5
2. Opening—Act I 11
3. Comedy Tonight 12
   —Fanfare 25
3a. Set The Scene 29
4. Love I Hear 30
5. Free 35
6. The House of Marcus Lycus 45
   — *Dance* 46
6a. The Courtesans' Exit 54
7. Lovely 55
8. Pretty Little Picture 61
9. Everybody Ought To Have A Maid 72
9a. — *1st Encore* 79
9b. — *2nd Encore* 82
10. I'm Calm 86
11. Impossible 90
12. Fanfares No. 1 96
13. Bring Me My Bride 97
14. Fanfares No. 2 106
14a. Finale — Act I 106

ACT II

15. Entr'acte 107
16. Opening — Act II 112
16a. Love Is Going Around 113
16b. Back To The Plot 114
16c. Free — Soldiers' Incidental No. 1 114
16d. — Soldiers' Incidental No. 2 117
17. That Dirty Old Man 120
18. That'll Show Him 126
19. *Reprise:* Lovely 130
20. Funeral Sequence 135
21. Incidental Chords 140
22. Finale Ultimo: Comedy Tonight 141
23. Curtain Calls 145
24. Exit Music 148

A FUNNY THING HAPPENED ON THE WAY TO THE FORUM

No.1   Overture

STEPHEN SONDHEIM

No. 2   Opening - Act I

Piano

Comedy Tonight

Cue: **PROLOGUS:** We shall employ every device we know in our desire to divert you. *(He gestures to the orchestra)*

PROLOGUS:

for - mal, Noth - ing that's nor - mal,

ALL:

No rec - i - ta - tions to re - cite! _____

O - pen up the cur - tain,

L'istesso tempo

PROLOGUS: It all takes place on a street in Rome, around and about these houses.

ALL:

Com - e - dy to - night!

PROLOGUS: First, the house of Erronius,.....etc
.... in search of his children.

Cls., 1 Tpt.

... stolen in infancy by pirates.

PROLOGUS:

Some-thing for ev-'ry-one, A com-e-dy to - night.

PROLOGUS: Second, the house of Lycus,
a....etc.....absolutely no
interest in pirates.

264

266

PROLOGUS: Raise the curtain! *
Vamp-ad lib.
(Br. 8va-1time only)

271 Cue: ...a role of enormous variety....
Tpt. solo (muted)

ff

p Str.

....Let me put it this way.. I play the part!

Hp.

279 (Sings)

An-y-thing you ask for.. Com-e-dy to-night!

W.W.

Str. rhythm

f Tutti

(Bs.8 bassa)

* Slide whistle
Timp.

A Roman ladder. Tremendous skill, incredible versatility. And above all, dignity! *(Segue)*

And now the entire company!

327

sempre cresc.

sempre cresc.

335

Tpts.

Trbs.

Br.

Fanfare

339 Vlns., W.W. 8va

fff

Br.

343

ALL:

Some-thing   fa - mil - iar,   Some-thing   pe - cu - liar,   Some-thing   for

Vlns., W.W. 8va

mf   Trbs., Vla., Cello

2nd HALF: ... **ALL:**

Cun-ning dis-guis - es, Hun-dreds of act-ors out of sight! _____

W.W. / f / Br. / Timp. roll

375

ERRONIUS: ... **SENEX:**

Pant-a-loons and tu - nics, Court-e-sans and eu-nuchs,

Tutti

DOMINA: ... **LYCUS:** ... **383** ... **PHILIA:** **HERO:**

Fu-ner-als and chas - es, Bar - i-tones and bass - es, Pan-der-ers, Phi-

HYSTERIUM: **MILES:** **LYCUS:** **ERRONIUS:** **PHILIA:** **DOMINA:**

lan-der-ers, Cu - pid-i - ty, Ti - mid-i - ty, Mis-takes, Fakes, Rhymes, Mimes,

391 Stately

PROLOGUS:

Tum-blers, grum-blers, fum-blers, bum-blers,

ALL:

No roy-al curse,

No Tro-jan horse,

And a hap-py end-ing, of course!

399

Good-ness and bad-ness, Man in his mad-ness, This time it all turns out all-right!

407 ALL: (Minus Prologus)

Trag-e-dy to-mor-row,

No. 3a

Set The Scene

Cue: PROLOGUS: The play begins.

SENEX: Slaves!

Love, I Hear

Cue: HERO turns to the audience.

Now that we're a-lone, — May I tell you I've been feel-ing ver - y strange? Ei-ther some-thing's in the air Or else a change is hap-pen-ing in me. — I think I know the cause, — I hope I know the cause. — From ev-'ry-thing I've heard There's on-ly one cause it can be.

Moderately - In 4

Love, I hear, ___ Makes you sigh a lot. Al - so,

love, I hear, ___ Leaves you weak. ___

Love, I hear, ___ Makes you blush and turns you ash - en. You

try to speak with pas - sion and squeak, I hear.

Love, they say, _____ Makes you pine a - way. But you pine a - way _____ With an id - i - ot - ic grin. _____ I pine, I blush, I squeak, I squawk. To - day I woke too weak to walk. What's love, I hear, I feel__ I fear I'm in.

Cue: HERO: You are free!

veg-'ta-ble un-less you're free! It's a lit-tle word but, Oh, the dif-

f'rence it makes! It's the nec-es-sa-ry es-sence of de-moc-ra-cy,— It's the

thing that ev-'ry slave should have the right to be.— And I soon will have the right to buy a

slave for me!— Can you see him? Well, I'll free him! When a

Cue: **PSEUDOLUS:** Show me, Lycus.
       LYCUS: Eunich! A buyer!

PSEUDOLUS: Don't you have anybody in there a bit less __ noisy?
LYCUS: I have. May I present <u>Panacea</u>. *(Segue)*

LYCUS: To make her available to you ... etc.
Vamp ad lib. ...and a body that stands behind
each promise. *(Segue)*

LYCUS: You are disturbed?   PSEUDOLUS: The proportions....etc
94 *Fade out as PSEUDOLUS says:* Yes, but how often will we find
ourselves in this position? Perhaps if we __ *(Fade out)*

Cue: LYCUS: No need to compromise __ Consider the Gemini __

101

Hp. solo (5 distinct glissandos)

Cue: A matched pair!

Vlns., Cl. 1

Gong (on cue)

107 W.W., Str.

Cls.   ad lib Hp. arpeggios

pp

Cello

Vla.

[*accel. e cresc. on cue*]

(Hp. arpeggios continue)

Bs.

Ped.   Ped.   Ped.

+Br.

Orch.   *ppp*
Harp continues after
Orch. stops

Cue: LYCUS:.... an infinite number of mathematical possibilities. *(Dialogue continues)*

... LYCUS: I couldn't. You understand.

PSEUDOLUS:
Completely.

LYCUS: Fortunately,
we still have
Vibrata.

Drs. *Vamp ad lib.*
a tempo

Bs., Celli, pizz.

113

Br. muted

Finger Cymb. *(Rhythm continues)*

LYCUS: Exotic as a desert bloom... etc.
... For the man whose interest is wildlife...

Vamp ad lib.

Drs.

VIBRATA:

Ee _____ Ee _____ Ay - ah, Ay -

Tpt. solo

mp Finger Cymb.

Saxs.

Bs.(pizz.)

VIBRATA:

ah! Ay_ Ay! Ee_____

PSEUDOLUS: Lycus, all that I can see is...etc.
LYCUS:...exactly what you want. May I present...
Gymnasia!

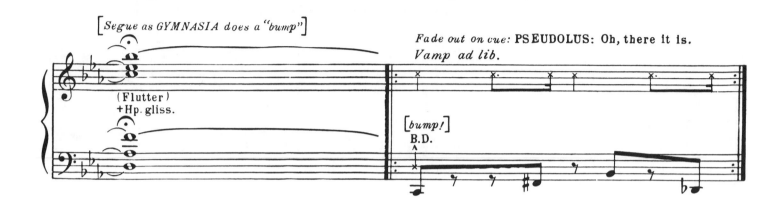

No. 6a

The Courtesans' Exit

Cue: LYCUS: Courtesans! Out of the sun and into the house.

No.7

Lovely

Cue: PSEUDOLUS: Don't worry. Nothing will happen. He's a virgin too.

Slowly-In 4

Fl.solo   PHILIA: My name is Philia.   *Dialogue continues.*

Piano

Cue: PHILIA: We are taught beauty...

PHILIA:

I'm

sew, Nor_ cook,_ nor read or write my name._____ But I'm

43

hap - py_____ Mere-ly be-ing love - ly,_____ For it's

one thing I can give to you._____

HERO: Philia. PHILIA: Yes?
HERO: Say my name. PHILIA: Just say your name?
HERO: Yes. PHILIA: Very well _ I have
forgotten it.
HERO: It's Hero. PHILIA: Forgive me, Hero. HERO: You don't need one.
I have no memory for names. You don't need anything. *Sings:*

Vamp ad lib. You're

R.H.

+muted Br.

Pretty Little Picture

Cue: PSEUDOLUS: **Far away.**

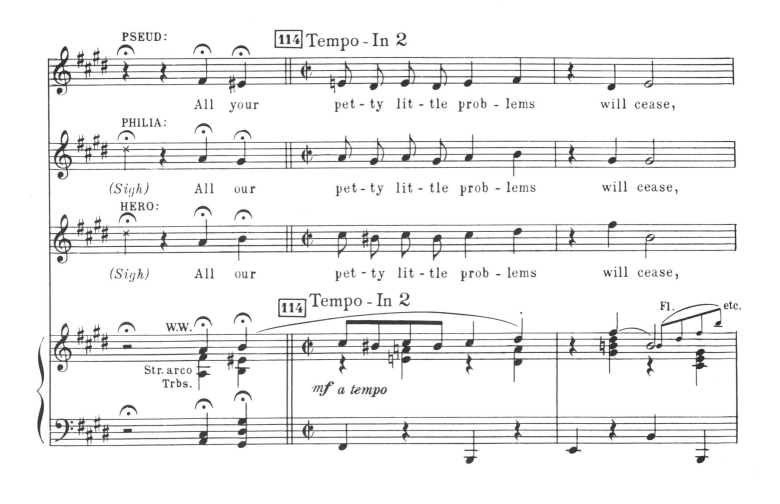

Pret - ty lit - tle pic - ture!

Pret - ty lit - tle pic - ture!

Pret - ty lit - tle pic - ture!

No.9 Everybody Ought To Have A Maid

Cue: SENEX: Maids like me. I'm neat.

26

Sweep-ing out? Sleep-ing in? Ev-'ry-bod-y ought to have a

maid! Some-one whom you hi-re when you're

PSEUDOLUS:

Ev-'ry-bod-y ought to have a maid!

short of help,_ To of-fer you_ the sort of help_ You

win-some as __ a whip-poor-will __ And grace-ful as a grouse.

Fl.,Cl.,Xyl.
mf
+Hp.
+Br.

107 **112**

Skit-ter-ing down the hall-way, Flit-ter-ing thru the par-lor,
Str.,W.W.,Hp.
+Tpts.

Tit-ter-ing in the pan-try, Lit-ter-ing up the bed-room, Put-ter-ing all a-round __
Tutti

The house! _____
f
Vla.,Cello,Trbs. tacet
ff Tutti
+Bs.

Applause - Segue

Everybody Ought To Have A Maid
Encore No. 1

Cue: HYSTERIUM taps PSEUDOLUS.

No. 9b

Everybody Ought To Have A Maid
Encore No. 2

Cue: *LYCUS in place.*

I'm Calm

Cue: **HYSTERIUM:** Calm? Calm? Mustn't get excited.

Impossible

Cue: **SENEX:** Pressing business.
(PHILIA appears on balcony)

Fanfares-No.1

No.13   Bring Me My Bride

Cue: **PSEUDOLUS: Perfect! I would like a mosaic of this scene. An entire wall made up of ‥**

PSEUDOLUS: Marcus Lycus, sir, I am dazzled by your presence.
MILES: Everyone is.
PSEUD: Welcome..... etc.
MILES: My bride!

MILES: You are?

(Last time)
My

bride! My bride! I've come to claim my bride. Come

ten-der-ly to crush her a-gainst my side! Let haste be made! I

can - not be de-layed! There are lands to con-quer, Cit-ies to loot And

Look at the size of those thighs, Like a might-y ma - chine!

PSEUDOLUS:
Those are the might-i-est thighs that I ev-er have theen! I mean.. My

MILES:

Str.,W.W.
Vlns. trem.
+Timp.

75

bride! My bride! In - form my luck-y bride: The
Vlns.
mf Cls.
+Trbs., Celli, B.Cl.

+Vlns.,Vla.

fa-bled arms of Mi - les are o-pen wide! Make haste! Make haste! I

Fanfares-No. 2

No. 14a

Finale - Act I

Cue: MILES: What now, Lycus?

[Curtain]

Entr'acte

No.16   Opening - Act II

Love Is Going Around

Cue: PROLOGUS: Welcome again, playgoers. You are about to witness the second half of our play. *(Signals orchestra)*

On cue: SENEX:... sow my last oat, if memory serves.   Fade and segue to No. 16 b

No. 16 b   Back To The Plot

Cue: SENEX: Let the play continue.

No. 16 c   Incidental
(Soldiers' Free)

Cue: COURTESANS exit into center house.

No. 16d   Incidental No. 2

Cue: HYSTERIUM:___ a house full of courtesans and a virgin on the roof!

* *Cue may be on repeat.*

That Dirty Old Man

Cue: DOMINA: ... you are talking to a woman who faces facts!

That'll Show Him

Cue: **PHILA:** And I have a way to make him suffer.

tent for two, I'll sit on his knee, —

Get to know him in - ti - mate - ly, — That - 'll show him

How much I real - ly love you! _____

Lovely - Reprise

Cue: **PSEUDOLUS: I can't take my eyes off you.**

love - ly, _____ That the world will nev - er seem _____ the

same.

PSEUD: Now, lie there, close your eyes and think dead thoughts.

Good! HYSTERIUM:

I'm love - ly, _____ Ab - so - lute - ly

love - ly, _____ Who'd be - lieve the love - li - ness of

No. 20

Funeral Sequence

Cue: MILES: Do not try to cheer me. I am inconsolable!

...MILES: I cannot afford to offend the Gods.
PSEUD: Who can? 54

Repeat ad lib.
MILES: *(Last time)*

All

Crete was at her feet, But I shall weep no more. I'll

Ah _____ Ah _____

92

find my con - so - la - tion as be - fore _____ A -

Ah   Ah   Ah ____   Ah ____

96   *molto rit.*

mong the sim - ple plea - sures of war! _____

Ah   Ah   Ah! ____

No. 21   Incidental Chords

Cue: **PSEUDOLUS.** The plague!   The plague!

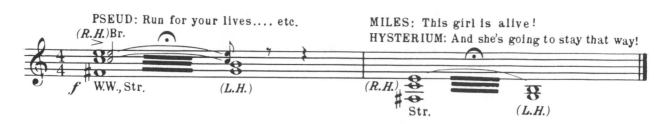

PSEUD: Run for your lives.... etc.   MILES: This girl is alive!

HYSTERIUM: And she's going to stay that way!

Finale Ultimo

No. 23

Curtain Calls

Exit Music